God Bless!

Lyn Holley Doucet

Water FROM Stones

AN INNER JOURNEY

LYN HOLLEY DOUCET

Acadian House
PUBLISHING
Lafayette, Louisiana

All scripture quotes used in this book were taken from *The New Jerusalem Bible*, New York: Doubleday and Co., Inc., 1990.

Library of Congress Cataloging-in-Publication Data

Doucet, Lyn Holley, 1950-
  Water from stones : an inner journey / by Lyn Holley Doucet.
     p. cm.
  Includes bibliographical references and index.
  ISBN 0-925417-40-8
  1. Spiritual life—Christianity. I. Title.
  BV4501.2 .D644 2001
  248.4—dc21
                    2001001789

- ♦ Published by Acadian House Publishing, Lafayette, Louisiana (Edited by Trent Angers; interior graphic design and production by Jon Russo)

- ♦ Cover illustration and inside illustrations by Regina Champagne Babin, Houma, Louisiana

- ♦ Cover design and production by Elizabeth Bell, Lafayette, Louisiana

- ♦ Poetry by Laurie Trumps, Lafayette, Louisiana

- ♦ Printed by Sheridan Books, Fredericksburg, Virginia

Introduction

Strike the rock, and water will come out for the people to drink.

(Exodus 17:6)

At age forty-five my friend Marion sat alone in a small townhouse surrounded by unpacked boxes. She felt frozen in disbelief. She would later describe the events leading up to this day as "a fire that consumed everything in my life."

In one short year Marion's twenty-year marriage had dissolved and her two beloved children had left home. The younger, David, had gone to boarding school and Rebecca, her seventeen-year-old, was living with an aunt. The year had begun with extreme rebelliousness on Rebecca's part that spiraled into severe health problems for the troubled girl. At one time these problems became life-threatening. Now Rebecca was facing an unplanned pregnancy. Jim, Marion's husband, had grown increasingly hurt, angry and controlling until Marion felt she had to leave their beautiful home and the life they shared.

Now she sat wondering, "How could all this happen?" Later she pondered, "What part did I play in this (seeming) disaster?"

Marion couldn't know that she now stood at the threshold of healing and spiritual growth, that the stones of her despair would yield the waters of transformation.

Three years after this gloomy day, I had lunch with Marion. She looked at me over her Italian salad and smiled.

"I really am just beginning to understand the devastation that happened in my life," she said. "But, you know, I am grateful. Those experiences have brought me to the place I am today. I'm not always thrilled with this address. Yet, I've grown so much."

Marion shared with me that through these experiences she had released much of the perfectionism that had become toxic to herself and others. She had turned her heart and her life over to God, for she saw no other choice. Like many of us, she had begun to give up her illusions of control and to accept and honor what *was*. As she returned to simplicity, she and her husband were able to begin seeing one another and communicating in productive ways. They achieved a beautiful reconciliation and remarriage.

Now Marion celebrates home, friends, and family in a new and profoundly grateful way. Her unexpected grandchild has become a source of love and joy. Perhaps because of Marion's healing, each family member began to take stock, to grow up, and to heal. As she ended her time in her desert of change Marion told me, "I feel blessed and much, much wiser."

When the Israelites traveled far into the desert, they became increasingly fearful, angry and petulant. They had thought that they were beginning a new life of freedom; now they feared death. All around them were the hard, rocky stones of the desert. And yet, just as they begged to return to their slavery, water gushed forth from the very stones of their torment. God chose this clear and commanding way to show them that they were not forgotten on their journey. God brought them to a renewed promise of life in a rich and fertile land. In this book, *Water From Stones*, you will read the stories of many people who have made desert journeys and found a new land, people just like you and me and my friend, Marion.

In the first section of this book, *Out of Egypt*, you will be asked to examine your life as it is today. Only you know which aspects of your life are stony, and which aspects promise a cool drink of living water. Where are you today? What changes in life are calling your name?

We are the same as the Israelites as we make our way: God has not forgotten us. In the stones that wound us, the waters of new life lie hidden. The life of the Spirit is within us and surrounding us, inviting us into a fully lived life of joy.

– Lyn Holley Doucet

How to use this book...

Water From Stones is intended to be used as an instrument of healing, renewal and enlightenment for those who are seeking to walk a spiritual path.

Hurt and disappointment are often a fact of life, a human reality. We are sometimes faced with a choice: Does this pain-filled event cause me to harden my heart, to numb my spirit? Or does it lead to growth and a greater sensitivity to my purpose in life? It is my hope that this book will be a tool that will help you to choose the life-giving path.

The following suggestions are intended to help you use this book more effectively.

First, set aside a special place to read, reflect and journal. For many people, it is a challenge to have a special place of one's own. If you do not have a room, try to find a quiet nook of some sort where you can surround yourself with things that give you comfort. In my special place, I have small stuffed animals and angel figures, as well as green plants. These things relax me and provide a connection to my inner world.

Second, set aside a specific time each day. For many, getting up a little earlier, perhaps with a cup of coffee, to read and journal in the morning quiet works well. For others, an after-supper time is the only possibility.

Third, purchase a journal or notebook with big enough pages for you to write without constraint. Have pens on hand that you enjoy using, pens that don't skip or splotch. Some people like to have colored pencils or colored felt-tip pens for drawing or underlining.

Fourth, go at your own pace. You may want to spend several days with some chapters. Reread the chapter as much as you like. If you do not care to use all the journaling topics, that is fine. Do what is best for you. Be careful, however, because sometimes what we really don't want to write about or think about is the subject with which we most need to deal. Write freely without censoring or editing your words.

Fifth, leave blank pages after your journaling topics to return to on "synthesis days" to write again, after you have read what you previously wrote. In a sense, you will be answering yourself as you gain greater clarity on issues.

Sixth, say the daily affirmation throughout your work with the book. The more it is said, the more it sinks into the conscious and subconcious mind. Be sure to repeat it just before going to bed.

Throughout the book I use the word "Spirit" as a synonym for God. My invitation is to think of God as creator, friend, Abba, life-giver, brother/sister, wisdom, the infinite. This is the God in whom we are immersed, the in-dwelling God who lives in our hearts.

I have written this book from a Christian perspective, which was formed from my religious background and practice. However, it is my hope that the book can be of help to a person of any faith who is on a spiritual journey.

My dear friend and spiritual partner, Donna Hayes, has taught me a most wonderful and useful mantra that I invite you to use throughout the process encountered in *Water From Stones*. It is, "Gently, Gently." Please be especially gentle with yourself and others as you work through this process. Take your time, and release your expectations of yourself and others. Let yourself just feel what you feel and be where you are. Be careful not to judge yourself or your "progress."

And remember that our God is a gentle, healing God of love who has all the time in the world.

– Lyn Holley Doucet

Suggestions for Group Use of *Water From Stones* and a related Prayer Ritual can be found toward the back of this book, beginning on page 115.

Dedicated to those who have claimed the courage to walk the spiritual path. May this book help you toward greater joy and peace.

Acknowledgements

This book came together with the help, support and encouragement of a number of people. I am indebted to all of them for their contributions.

• The focus group who helped me survey then structure the material for the book, namely, Donna Hayes Huval, Sharane Gott, Trudy Gomez, Cle'lie Senne, Laurie Trumps and Sharon O'Neill.

• All of those who so generously shared the personal stories that bring life to the principles offered in these pages.

• The readers who reviewed and critiqued the manuscript prior to publication: Fr. Keith LaBove, Nancy Ehret, Pat Lowe, Deanna Fouin, Vic & Rose Hummert, Rev. Diane Moore and Neal Bertrand.

• The editors, Sarah Moss, who did the preliminary editing and truly helped me to birth this project; and Trent Angers, who did the finishing work with great care and endless patience.

• My parents, Minnetta and J.B. Holley, who led me to a great love of words and knowledge; my husband, Dee Doucet, who has filled my life with abundance and love; my sisters, Minnett and Judy, and my brother, Boyd, who have helped to shape my life in positive ways; and my son, Jacques, who has filled my heart with joy and laughter.

• Two special friends who have always been there for me, Dale & Ginger Doucet.

• The women of Le Papillon Theresians Group, whose prayers and support were welcomed and felt throughout this project.

Table of Contents

(Continued on next page)

Part III: *Stumbling Stones*

Part IV: *A New Land*

Water
FROM Stones

Gather us in, the lost and forsaken;
Gather us in, the blind and the lame.
Call to us now, and we shall awaken;
We shall arise at the sound of our name.

(From *Gather Us In*, by Marty Haugen)

PART I

OUT OF EGYPT

Chapter One

Thriving Now

Moses was looking after the flock of his father-in-law,
Jethro.   (Exodus 3:1)

F or most of us, life isn't filled with high drama and a
burning bush, but with the details of the life we
have been given, the life of the here and now.

Sometimes as we tend our flocks, whether at home or in the
workplace, we feel a great sense of contentment. At other times,
we are indeed in the desert. To begin positive change in our lives
is to learn to thrive now, to live with gratitude, moment by moment, day by day.

One beautiful day in early spring, as I took a walk in the country, I passed an old, deserted home-place. The house was gone,
but on the grounds live oaks stood stately and green, daffodils
fluttered their creamy yellow blossoms and azaleas burst with color.
An exuberant wisteria vine spread its rich purple flowers over a
weathered fence. For me, the scene gave new meaning to the

folksy saying, "Bloom where you are planted." It made me smile to think that God's creation does not require an audience or a perfect environment to be exquisitely beautiful. With this in mind, it seems to me that if we are firmly resolved to thrive *here and now*, we can plant the seeds of positive change in our own lives.

To do this we need to live in gratitude, releasing our rigid expectations of how our lives should be. To develop gratitude, we begin by being awake and observant. I cannot celebrate the good things in my life if I do not open my eyes to see them carefully in each moment. Gratitude also means that I view life as a gift – and that I do not refuse the gift because all the details are not up to my expectations. Fixed expectations can blind us to the good that is fully present *now*.

If we think about this issue of expectations, we will find many examples in our own lives. This mindset of "just wanting what we want" makes it easy to miss the beauty that is present all around us.

In *Quest for God*, Paul Johnson writes:

"The universe is so full of beauty that it is difficult for one limited human being to take it all in.... God is, if anything, too generous...."

This beauty lies not only in the natural world, but also in God's creative power, which is constantly at work in our lives.

For Journaling and Reflection...

1. Write about several aspects of your life for which you are grateful. (Don't forget the little things like a hummingbird feeder or good coffee in the morning, or the big things like a good marriage or a faithful best friend.)

2. What factors (spiritual reading, church, support groups, nature) in your life help you to thrive spiritually? Journal about them and how they contribute to your spiritual well-being.

3. Are expectations of "how things should be" a challenge for you?

4. How do you cope with disappointment in your life?

Affirmation: *God is with me in this moment.*

Chapter Two

OUR ROLES

There are many ways we are called to come home to ourselves. — Macrina Wiederkehr

A friend of mine, Sarah, told me about her struggles with her job. It required sixty hours a week from her. She often had to work at night, and she dealt with angry people on a daily basis. She had a number of bosses who often did not agree. She could see the toll her job was taking on her, emotionally, spiritually and physically.

On the other hand, her salary was excellent. She felt that, as a single woman, she needed all of her income, and she enjoyed being able to make decisions and to help people.

"I can't leave my job! I *am* my job!" she said to me in summary.

This statement stunned me a little, and I felt somewhat smug for a moment. After all, I knew that I wasn't *my* job. But then I thought:

"Who *would* I be if I were not a mother, wife, daughter, sister, speech therapist, struggling musician and struggling writer? Would I just disappear?"

In this life, we acquire many roles. These roles may fit well with our unique personalities and destinies – or they may not. Sometimes clinging to them is destructive. Often, our ego demands that we cling, in perceived safety, to the very roles that are hurting us. Many people stay in terrible and even life-threatening relationships. Why do they stay? Often, it is fear that makes them prefer "the devil that they know" instead of "the devil that they don't know."

How many people complain bitterly about their work, but make absolutely no plans to change anything? Could they get training to allow them to move up or move on? Could they make some real changes in their current job that they are afraid to make? The point here is not to judge others, but to pose some questions:

How is clinging because of fear present in *my* life? Are there things I need to begin to change? People or things that I need to accept? Ideally our roles enhance our true self rather than hiding or disfiguring it. (Remember to be gentle with yourself as you examine your roles.)

Some roles are subtle, but very defining. Priscilla, a teacher, discovered that she was doing things for family members that they should be doing for themselves, leaving her exhausted. It took a serious injury to force her to change her "over-doing."

Another woman I know, Joan, had to exit her role as friend

when she realized that her best friends were chronically depressed, unwilling to seek help and making her more depressed, too! These friends had many unpleasant things to say about Joan as she pulled away, and this made change very difficult.

My buddy, Michael, a talented musician, decided to reexamine his long-term dislike of organized religion. He wanted to serve God in his music, and he felt called to do so in a church setting. He became a liturgical musician and has never regretted his decision.

As our roles change, begin and end, we can be propelled to seek again that original self that is truly "us," the child of God.

For Journaling and Reflection...

1. List two or three roles with which you identify (for example, mother, teacher and friend). Describe some activities associated with these roles. Another way to put this is, "How do these roles affect my daily life?"

2. Which of these roles is most energy-draining? Why?

3. Which roles seem to come easier to you and/or are most life-giving? Why?

4. If you were given magical powers, what would you change about your roles?

Affirmation: *I am finding my way.*

Chapter Three

THE EGO, THE SELF
AND AUTHENTICITY

*We have the illusion that we can control events if we
do everything right.*   — Rabbi Kushman

As we continue to move toward the desert, let us take
a day or so to explore some terms that we need for
our trip. Often, when we speak about psychological terms, we
forget that they are just concepts, clusters of definitions.

Moreover, these terms can be used in different ways by different authors. For our purposes, the ego can be thought of as our
executive function. It keeps us organized and helps us to achieve
goals. It is the "me" that we usually present to others. We need
a strong and well-functioning ego in order to live well in the
world. In my work as a teacher I have met little children whose
egos have been stomped nearly to death. They have no bound-
aries and no sense of who they are. The ego is an expression of

consciousness and often represents the values and mores of our parents, our religion, and our society.

Problems with the ego begin when it works actively to keep us *where we are*. The ego craves safety and fears risk. Therefore, maintaining the *status quo* is often a goal of the ego, even when this goal may not serve our highest interests. The ego has pretty much decided that we *are* what we do and how we look. If people approve of us, the ego is usually happy (for a short period, until it is time to earn more approval).

Within the ego are pride, perfectionism, and resistance to change and even to God's will, if it does not match our agenda. So even though the ego keeps us efficient and organized, it may keep us miserable and false as well!

In the book, *Discovering The Enneagram*, Andreas Ebert writes:

"In Christianity redemption from the false self is understood as a gift of God's grace."

Through prayer and awareness we can find the humility to be fully open to this grace and to move from an ego-controlled "false self" to a more conscious, free and loving "true self."

Some psychologists identify the *self* as the portion of our psychological make-up that contains "the God within." At its best, the self speaks for God and for our highest good. We become authentic when we act from "self."

A friend of mine was reminiscing about raising her children, and she told me she had three little ones close together and that she felt overwhelmed.

"I kept running to workshops and reading books," she said. "I felt that others had all the answers and I had none! Now I think that I had everything I needed. I just didn't know it. I wouldn't be quiet and still long enough to look into my own heart."

Her story demonstrates that by taking the time and seeking the quiet to look into our own hearts, we can find our authentic selves. We are born with the potential to develop all the wisdom we need. Often, practicing our inner wisdom means going against the opinions of others and doing what we feel is right. This sounds easy but can be very painful. Those who dare to write, to paint, to leave, to stay and to disagree are given power to do so by listening to the self. With God's help, we can become authentic: the person we were always meant to be.

Sometimes, however, the self becomes lost and overpowered by the ego. It often takes an illness, a depression, or some loss to force the ego to surrender control. When we reflect now about journeys across the desert, and bruisings upon the rocks, we are often speaking of just such times of ego surrender. Only when our own agendas are released will God rise up in the self and save us with the waters of life.

For Journaling and Reflection...

1. Do the concepts of "ego" and "self" have meaning for you? How do you experience the ego within? (You may want to reread this section about the characteristics of ego.)

2. If "self" is the authentic person within, how would you describe your "self"? Are you kind? Creative? Playful? Serious? Spend some time thinking about the real you. You may want to think about yourself as a child and remember and journal about your childhood personality characteristics.

3. At what times in your life today do you most fully feel "yourself"?

Affirmation: *I perceive my true self.*

Chapter Four

RELATIONSHIPS

*She had truly been a "love song" of God for the
many people she had touched.... Her life (was) not
grandiose ... but out of those ordinary activities she
had brought an extraordinary song of love to others.*
                                        – Joyce Rupp

*M*y childhood Christmas memories are filled with
the excitement of seeing my grandmother and grand-
father drive up in their big car, always with a trunk full of Christmas gifts for me and my siblings.

We would all receive homemade sock monkeys of every sort –
little boys and girls dressed in hats and striped overalls or frilly
dresses and bows. Grandmother loved to knit sweaters for us for
Christmas. She would put together the most amazing color com-
binations! When we unwrapped the presents she would say, "Now,
you can wear that with orange pants or maybe a red skirt or
blue pants." My grandmother colored my Christmases with her

unconditional love.

In the life of my grandmother, I see my own call to creativity. In my writing space at home, I have hung a painting done by her in the 1960s or '70s – a copper vase filled with zinnias of every color. It serves to remind me of her creative spirit as I write. We are so much alike, yet different. She loved color, and so do I. She loved to learn how to do new things and could laugh when her projects didn't turn out so well. (I usually don't.)

"Just do the best you can," she would say.

For many of us, important lessons will be learned in relationships with others all through our lives. We can see our faults and our strengths clearly mirrored in other people. When I am feeling well and optimistic, it seems relatively easy to be in a happy relationship with friends and family. When I am ill, tired or disappointed, people can seem insensitive. And I have come to realize how insensitive I can be to others, as I remain locked up tight in my own life.

Relationships give us the grounding that we need in order to travel a spiritual path. Even those who lived solitary lives, such as the writer May Sarton, relied on letters and visits from beloved friends to help them make sense of the world. These relationships take many forms: husband or wife, child, teacher, mentor, friend, student, parent, grandparent, colleague. Each one brings a special flavor to our lives and special challenges as well.

Ideally, relationships point us to God, the source of perfect love. Yet, relationships have their stones, their deserts and, yes, their waters of life. I know that when I am in the rocky throes of an argument with my husband I feel only pain. Only later can I reflect upon his point of view. (Okay, I admit it! Sometimes I refuse to reflect on his point of view!) Love doesn't always feel wonderful, yet love can teach us many things about ourselves.

As we release rigid ideas of perfect relationships, and as we forgive, we grow much wiser.

For Journaling and Reflection...

1. Discuss two or more major relationships in your life, past and present, journaling in detail.

2. In which of these relationships were you or are you most free to be yourself? Why?

3. Which of these relationships has been the most difficult? Why?

4. What relationships in your life have caused you to grow spiritually? Why?

Affirmation: *May I grow in love.*

Chapter Five

GOD'S LOVE:
OUR BIRTHRIGHT

*God continues to walk with us and teach us, to embrace
us when we succeed and pick us up when we fail.*

          – Virginia Ann Froehle

*W*hen Denrell first came into my speech therapy office he was a little boy of five, and he was in trouble. He was abused and neglected at home and was unable to cope with the demands of school.

His large, dark eyes were sad, like those of an abandoned puppy. He didn't smile very often, but when he did his smile transformed his face and lit his sensitive eyes.

He pulled his chair close to me, and I put my arm around him. He nestled his head into my side. Often, we would sit like this for half of the therapy session. I would say affirming things to him.

"You are a good boy, Denrell. We all care about you. You are safe here," I would tell him.

Much time passed, and our relationship deepened. I had never invested so much of my heart into a student before, and it hurt. Often, Denrell would cry and cling to his teacher or me when it was time to catch the bus for home. Our principal's many home visits and calls to social service agencies produced no results. Denrell's abuse was not visible on the outside, but it was destroying him on the inside. I was always trying to learn more about him.

"Let's name all of the people who love you," I said to Denrell.

He was pleased with this task and listed for me his principal, the counselor, his teacher and then, softly, his mommy. I replied that, yes, all these people loved him. Then I said, "God loves you."

His eyes got very big, and he pointed a finger skyward as he said, "God?"

"Yes," I replied (wondering if I was breaking some public school law, and not really caring if I was). "You are special to God, and God cares about what happens to you. He is always near and you can talk to him. You are his child."

"God loves me," Denrell said softly as he snuggled back into my side.

Privately, I struggled with my own doubts, as I always did. Why was there so much suffering by the innocent in this world? Why didn't God step in and fix some of these terrible situations? I knew that these questions involve our free will and can never be fully answered here on earth. I also knew that God's love is our birthright – mine and yours, and Denrell's.

In Denrell's suffering and longing for love, I saw my own inner struggle to fit into this world. If I could feel such strong love for Denrell, then what of God's love for me? If a mere human being can respond with so much compassion, then I could be sure that I was loved, fully. I was accepted with tenderness by God despite my many imperfections.

In my weak and limited way, I longed to bring healing to Denrell. How much more does God in his great compassion yearn to reach us? With God's help, we can bring into full maturity those parts of ourselves that are still lost in childhood.

For Journaling and Reflection...

1. Describe yourself as a child of eight or so. Can you remember much about yourself? What traits stand out in your personality at that age? (Were you trusting? Fearful?)

2. Journal about your first impression of God. (Was God the judge? The Good Shepherd?) Who shared ideas about God with you when you were a child? Describe this person or persons.

3. Have your views about God changed? If so, why have they changed?

4. How are you able to feel God's love in your life? Through others? At church? In nature? Journal about these feelings, people and/or places.

Affirmation: *I am perfectly loved by God.*

Chapter Six

SYNTHESIS

Let each season encircle all the other seasons, and let today embrace the past with remembrance and the future with longing.   – Kahlil Gibran

*I*n giving ourselves the gift of looking at our lives as they are now, we are pleasing God, who said, "Love others as you love yourself."

As we look at thriving and being grateful now – and at our roles, relationships, egos and "true selves" – we gain valuable knowledge about how we want to live our lives and how we *can* live them to the fullest.

Begin now to notice recurring themes, in the book itself or in your journal, that seem to be especially significant for you. Spend as much time as you need in meditation, journaling and prayer about these issues.

For Journaling and Reflection...

Read over your journal pages for this first section of the book. If you feel called to do so, reply in writing to your journaling. You may want to continue writing about the issues or insights that you find important at this time.

Affirmation: *God is in control.*

Change of Season

I sit upon my little porch,
Watching the line of summer trees,
Their colors softening to rust and brown.
What is dying?

Little by little, the wind will blow leaves away,
Now, the tree does not resist,
Deep within it, a gathering.
What will live?

I sit, knowing not the colors I should wear,
Maybe I will clash with the world.
Help me to gather,
And, oh, help me to let go.

— Lyn Holley Doucet

PART II

·

INTO THE DESERT

Chapter Seven

DESERT OF CHANGE

Why did we not die at Yahweh's hand in Egypt, where we used to sit round the flesh pots and could eat to our heart's content! As it is, you have led us into this desert to starve this entire assembly to death!

(Exodus 16:3)

We come now to the heart of our pilgrimage: our entering into the desert of change. In the chapters that follow we will discover some of the reasons why this desert experience occurs, and the ways in which others have traversed these rocky paths.

While I am serving as a sort of leader for this expedition, I, too, am learning as I go, as you will see from the following story. One night, when I was in the middle of writing this book, I had a dream that I was trying to get to a convention of some sort. A very young man was leading me in his car. He seemed to have no idea where he was going. He kept running off the side of the road as he drove into the darkness at a high rate of speed.

To make matters worse, my clothes were in disarray. I had on layers of clothing, and each layer was either ripped, stained or inappropriate for the convention.

When I awoke, I said to myself, "Oh, great! I'm trying to lead people through the desert, and I'm lost and my clothes are inappropriate!"

As we journey into the unknown, the part of ourselves that seeks the authentic life is like the teenager in my dream: filled with energy and the willingness to try, yet not filled with wisdom. We are souls who are young and lost. We stumble in the desert place, the new place, having left behind the familiar. Our clothes are truly not appropriate. We suffer humiliation and frustration as we try to find our new place, our *authenticity*. A friend of mine hit the nail on the head when she said:

"The desert is a dry, barren place where we keep planting and nothing seems to grow."

As we discussed earlier, the reason many people never venture out – even in their misery – is that it is too scary. There is too much of the unknown. It is so much easier to stay in the world we have always known, even if we are in a sort of bondage.

The Israelites had seen the wonders of God's hand. God had, miraculously, parted the waters of the Red Sea and had already purified some water for them to drink. Yet, when the wilderness threatened them, they begged to go back into slavery.

Sometimes we are cast into the wasteland through circumstances of our lives. Our expectations are shattered and our hearts are broken. In other cases, we must *choose* the desert in order to grow. In neither case is the wilderness an easy place to be. Yet, the desert is not a place of punishment but rather a place of purification. We must stop! We must wait! The desert takes away the distracting *desserts* so that we can find the real meaning of our lives.

In the book, *What Ever Happened to the Real Me?*, author Neva Coyle writes of loosening her bonds with the small, tightly knit church group of which she was a member. The ladies of this church met often for coffee klatches, and they would spend hours talking on the phone. They rarely saw others outside the group. Neva felt her perspectives shrinking. She wrote:

"The more I engaged in being the acceptable, presentable person, the less I was able to maintain any sense of being myself."

As she separated from the group, she could find no middle ground. She was alone. In her bruising desert time, she felt "abandoned and lonely." But, as she stayed her course, the great waters of her creativity sprang forth, and she became a noted author and speaker. She found her *self*.

A friend of mine described an experience of depression as being similar to entering the dark, constricting birth canal. In her journal she wrote:

"(Lord) I am so grateful that you allowed me not to be totally fearful of my depression and to trust that it was you walking me through it. I sense that I am in the birth canal of this present birth. I say 'present' because I know that there will be more deaths and rebirths in my life.... I am ready for perhaps my first real rebirth."

During the days to come, we will follow others into the desert of change, into the rebirthing process. We want to discover the waters of blessing that spring forth in their wilderness. We want to taste and see their new life. As we travel with them, it is my prayer that as your stones become known to you so will your hope and your springs in the desert.

For Journaling and Reflection...

1. Do you like or dislike change? Why?

2. If you fear certain changes, what specifically are your fears?

3. Reread the story of Neva Coyle. Can you remember any similar times in your life when you had to "choose the desert"? What happened?

4. Are you facing any changes in your life at this time? List each change, describing your feelings about each one.

Affirmation: *God will never abandon me!*

Chapter Eight

Janet's Story

*They then traveled through the desert for three days without finding
water. When they reached Marah, they could not drink the Marah
water because it was bitter.... Moses appealed to Yahweh for help.*

(Exodus 15:22-25)

*J*anet, a friend of mine, was contented with her life until an event occurred that dramatically changed it. Her beloved brother, only forty-six years old, died of a heart attack in a far-away country.

His sudden death shattered Janet and her entire family. Her brother had died alone; the family hadn't been able to say goodbye.

It was a loss that cut into the very fabric of Janet's life and faith, leaving her lost and confused. Tears flowed from her eyes constantly, and she found it hard to go about her daily routine. Everything seemed to remind her of her brother. She constantly asked the heavens, "Why? Why?"

During this time, Janet was given a little blue book called *Pieta*, which contained some ancient prayers of the church. She was able to identify strongly with the sufferings of Mary and of Christ. She began to set aside half an hour daily to pray, especially for her brother. She clung to the words printed in the little blue book, as her mind could form no words. Her husband respected her special time of prayer, when she would retreat to a small, screened porch in the back part of their home.

"May the fruit of thy suffering be renewed in my soul by the faithful remembrance of your passion, and may thy love increase in my heart each day," she prayed.

Gradually, she fixed up the small porch as a peaceful sanctuary, with fresh paint, rocking chairs, plants and a place for books. She began to notice the beauty of her backyard, the old oaks adorned with ferns that graced her property, the doves and the playful squirrels that visited daily.

Janet now identifies, in a much deeper way, with the pain of others. In her meditations, she has realized that much of life is outside her control, and she has learned to face this truth without bitterness. Now she can compassionately share with others in their grief.

For my friend, written prayers, washed in antiquity, have been a lifeline, a path to God. Through them, she has been able to break through her deepest darkness into a new light. In clinging to her time of solitude and prayer, with God's help she has claimed her own healing.

For Journaling and Reflection...

1. Have you experienced a time of deep loss in your life? Journal about it. What gifts came from this experience?

2. Will your faith allow you to see death as your return to a loving God?

3. Does solitude appeal to you, and do you spend time alone? If so, what is this like for you?

4. Are there certain prayers or practices that bring healing to your heart? Do you perform them often? Why or why not?

Affirmation: *God is healing my heart.*

Chapter Nine

KATHERINE'S STORY

A not admitting of the wound
Until it grew so wide
That all my life had entered it
And there were troughs beside
          – Emily Dickinson

*K*atherine smiles as she speaks of being reared in a "typically dysfunctional" family. There were many children in the home and not very much money. Her father was away from home a great deal, as a salesman, and her mother drank.

"It's funny, though," says Katherine. "I always felt loved. I had a sense of who I was supposed to be, and that kept me out of trouble."

Katherine was closest to her father and secretly felt that she was his favorite child. She admired him – his hard work, his neatness, his perfectionism with the yard, his sense of humor.

Time passed, Katherine grew up, and her mother received treatment for her addiction. Her parents drifted apart, and though they did not divorce they began to live separate lives.

Katherine married and started a career. Her father lived in a town nearby. Katherine found herself increasingly obsessed with the idea of having a close relationship with him. At the same time, she began to realize that the idealized father of her childhood never existed. She saw that her father manipulated others and even lied. Yet, rarely did an hour go by that Katherine did not think about him. Her life was becoming a wilderness filled with shadowy images of her father.

Katherine had long known that he had a girlfriend, although he never said a word about it. She began to gather bits of information about the relationship from others, including the fact that this lady had a dog by the name of "Buster."

One Saturday, Katherine was on the phone with her father. He explained that he had to stay home by himself and clean his house that day, rather than come to visit her. Suddenly, in the background, she heard the clear sound of a dog barking. Her father did not have a dog. She said good-bye and left her living room to walk down the hall to her bedroom.

"I will never forget what happened next," she relates. "I was literally struck down to my knees in the hall and could not get up. A firm but loving voice spoke to me, saying, 'Katherine, let your father go!'"

As she tells the story, laughter mingles with tears.

"I had no choice in the matter. At that moment, I let my father go to lead his own life as he saw fit. I am no longer controlled by his choices. I realized I couldn't fix my childhood or him," she explains.

Since that day, her healing has continued. Katherine's marriage and career have flourished. She has loving friends. Her relationship with her father is still far from perfect, but she is at peace. She knows that God has set her feet on a better path.

For Journaling and Reflection...

1. Write down your feelings about Katherine's desire to control her father.

2. Are there certain people whom you try to control? Are there people who try to control you?

3. If you have relationships that are undergoing change, journal about these relationships.

Affirmation: *God cares for me and for all those I love.*

Chapter Ten

A WELL IN THE DESERT

*...no one who drinks the water that I shall give will
ever be thirsty again. The water that I shall give will
become a spring of water within, welling up for
eternal life.* (John 4:14)

*W*hen I consider the meeting of Jesus with the Samaritan woman at the well, I think of their eyes: Jesus' eyes, tender, yet commanding; her eyes, at first, filled with disbelief and defensiveness, with a touch of derision. She asks:

"How can you, a Jew, be talking to me? How can you get water? You don't even have a rope or a bucket."

Then her eyes change; now comes a look of surprise, then hope, then amazement. Jesus tells her all about her life; yet, he has never met her before. He speaks with the authority of a great prophet, yet with real warmth.

In this powerful encounter, we can imagine a well made of rock, a dusty road, a woman in flowing garments, the brown stone jar she carried. Jesus would look tired, but would be fully engaged with this person whom he has encountered.

The fact that she is a Samaritan is one of the multiple strikes against her, in the eyes of the Jewish world. She is an unmarried woman, yet she is living with a man. Jesus ministers to this very woman to make a point: No one is excluded from the kingdom.

At this moment, frozen in time, when her feet are bruised by the rocky road and her heart is heavy, the Samaritan woman encounters the truth: Living water is available even to *her*. Jesus shows not only mercy but also loving respect; he gives her a reason to live, to hope.

When the woman hears the good news, she leaves her water jar and runs to tell others. In the book, *A Tree Full of Angels*, the author makes an important point:

"This very well may be the heart of this beautiful story. Her water jar was her own agenda."

She was willing to stop and listen. She was willing to be open to the good news Jesus brought; otherwise, his words would have fallen barren onto the desert sand. Instead, because of her openness to a new message, she received the water that we are still drinking today.

When you and I are willing to set aside our own agendas, our expectations and our fixed ways of seeing, we can be blessed beyond our wildest dreams. We can even be a source of living water (truth, hope, joy, love) for others.

I like to muse upon the fact that when this woman left her

home in the morning to go to the well, as she always did, she had no idea that this would be a life-changing day. And so it is with us.

When the road is sad and treacherous, don't despair; living water may gush forth in a most unexpected way. We should speak carefully to those we meet; we should listen closely. God may be sending us help!

For Journaling and Reflection...

1. Imagine that you are the Samaritan woman. Write down some specific questions that you would like to ask Jesus about your life: How does Jesus answer?

2. How are you thirsty? Are you lonely? Are you depressed or ill? Are you uncertain about relationships or change at work or at home?

Affirmation: *God is sending help.*

Chapter Eleven

A SCENE FROM
MY OWN DESERT

Going in white and blue, in Mary's colour...
Who then made the fountains and made fresh the springs...
Made cool the dry rock and made firm the sand
- T. S. Elliot

*N*ow, I write about one of the most precious events in my life. It seems strange to do so, as I have rarely told the story and have never written it down. The memory seems almost like a rare photographic negative that cannot be exposed to light, lest it be lost.

When I had been married for about fifteen years, I had much for which to be thankful. I had a loving husband, who provided well for us, and a wonderful nine-year-old son, Jacques, who had come to us after four years of treatment for my infertility. I was so thrilled to become pregnant, and I always knew that Jacques was a wonderful gift from God.

As the years passed, I very much wanted another child. I continued treatment, swallowing all sorts of pills, undergoing a surgery, constantly taking my temperature and suffering other humiliations that so many infertile women know about. Nothing happened! The day came when my doctor in Lafayette advised me to go to Houston to see a specialist, as he had no other help to offer me. I had seen other friends do this, and I felt it would be too much of a strain on my family and myself. It seemed that the door of hope was closing.

At about that same time, my very best friend and neighbor became pregnant with her second child. I descended into envy and depression.

One night, feeling very miserable, angry and depressed, I was reading a book called *Paying Attention to God*, by a Jesuit priest. In this book, the author explained that God already knew our hearts. If we were trying to protect God by sparing him our anger toward him, we were just blocking the relationship.

"Tell God exactly how you feel!" the author urged.

I had been given permission by a Jesuit priest, so I really "let God have it!" I screamed and cried out my anger, explaining that I was a good mother. I would take good care of another child. Why were all these other people able to have children and I was not? Unfit people were constantly having children!

What happened next is what makes this story so difficult to tell. I can only approximate the experience in words. Quite suddenly, I felt as though I was surrounded by a rich, luminous darkness. I fell deep into the chasm of this darkness, and it surrounded and enfolded me. I was at once awed and comforted being in this place that was not of this world. This magnificent sea of love and comfort was God, and from it came a voice that said, "I love your Lyn-ness."

I was filled with the most profound peace and light that I have ever experienced. The peace and light lasted, strongly, for three days. During that time, I offered love, peace and apology to those (including my best friend) to whom I had been beastly during my sad time.

As I write this, I am filled, once again, with some of the awe I discovered on that night. I encountered a God who did not need more children from me in order to love me. He already loved my very essence, my "Lyn-ness." I was not a failure. Since that night I have never doubted that there is a loving God, even when I do not understand God's ways.

For Journaling and Reflection...

1. Is there an area of your life in which you have experienced a major disappointment, perhaps a loss of faith? (A betrayal? Health problem? Loss of a good friend?)

2. How do you handle pain and disappointment in your life? Do you hide it? Vent it? Can you journal about some positive ways to process pain, loss and disappointment?

3. How has God touched you in special ways?

Affirmation: *God loves me as I am.*

Chapter Twelve

SYNTHESIS

Do not discount what you have already accomplished.
You have made important steps toward the freedom
you are searching for. – Henry Nouwen

*S*ome of the largest stones that bruise our feet are those of our own expectations. Because we expect things to be a certain way, we heap misery upon ourselves and others when they are not. We cannot "see" other ways of living.

I expected to be able to have as many children as I wanted; Katherine expected to maintain the fantasy father of her childhood; the woman at the well anticipated that all of society's rules would remain in place, even though they kept her on society's lowest rung.

When our fixed ideas of "the way things ought to be" begin to die (as they must), then we can soften our resistance to the desert journey. We can learn to embrace reality and God's will. With time and prayer our period of testing can ripen into a beautiful new beginning for us – our own small or large resurrection, a taste of Easter. Poet May Sarton says it well in *Easter Morning*:

The extreme delicacy of this Easter morning,
Spoke to me as a prayer, and as a warning.
It was light on the brink, spring light,
After a rain that gentled my dark night.
I walked through landscapes I had never seen.
Where the fresh grass had just begun to green.

The desert is a place where expectations are turned upside-down – and the ego is forced to surrender its death grip on our lives. When this happens, the holy water flows into us and new growth begins.

Some of us choose the desert when we feel we must change our lives. But choosing the desert does not necessarily make the time in the wasteland less lonely or dry.

The desert serves its purpose, when we learn the lessons that it can teach. Deep within us, in our wise inner self, the truth is released. The lessons are clarified and the gifts of the desert are received in abundance.

For Journaling and Reflection...

Read over your journal notes for the week and reflect about them. Spend as much time as you need in reflection and prayer concerning any issues that have been raised for you. Be gentle and loving toward yourself.

Affirmation: *Lord, it is you I follow.*

Cold Desert Morning

I've memorized it:
The way
You whispered once
My name,
Like it was a mysterious
Fragile living thing.

It was in your whisper
That I heard
The sound
Of my name,
As though, for the first time,
It echoed,
Held firmly
Against your chest,
In your stillness.

My name
Moved,
New and pure,
Through me
In just the way
The fog moves off the mesa,
On cold, clear desert mornings.

— Laurie Trumps

PART III

STUMBLING STONES

Chapter Thirteen

JUDGMENTS

I think that our society is a difficult place to live.
— Thich Nhat Hanh

$\mathcal{I}$f our journey through the wilderness took place on smooth, level ground we might make our trip quickly and with little pain. Unfortunately, all along the way we encounter attitudes within ourselves that impede our progress. I call these attitudes "stumbling stones."

The first such "stone" I will discuss is our proclivity to judge ourselves and others, usually in a harsh manner. The following story illustrates a lesson I learned about such judgments.

One day in the school where I worked time seemed to stand still as a kindergarten teacher rushed in with a small girl in her arms. The child was in the throes of a grand mal seizure, unaware of what was happening to her.

We laid her gently on the floor and called 911. She seemed to be having trouble breathing.

"Could she have swallowed something, like a quarter?" another teacher cried as she cradled the little girl's head.

The child continued to be rigid and unknowing, her dark eyes dilated, writhing in the seizure that seemed to go on for hours, although only minutes had passed. We were helpless, except to loosen clothing and whisper words of comfort. When the paramedics came, they rushed her to the hospital.

The incident was poignant for me, because this was a very mischievous little girl. She was not doing well in kindergarten, partly because she rarely paid attention and constantly thought of ways to get out of the room. At one time, during a staff meeting, I questioned whether or not she was manipulative. I felt very annoyed with her.

Now, I saw clearly that she was a baby, an innocent child of God. As she struggled for breath, her fragility and vulnerability tore at my heart. As I knelt on the floor and helplessly tried to minister to her, I knew I would never forget this day and the love I felt for her. My change of heart reminded me that my perspective is not always "the truth" and that my critical nature can prevent me from being compassionate.

As we release our harsh judgments of others we can begin to release them toward ourselves. This does not mean that we must accept what is evil in the world. Heaven forbid!

There is a big difference between discernment and judgment. In discernment, which is really thoughtful analysis, we may decide that a person is not acting in his/her own or others' best interests. This is opposed to judgment that, consciously or not, labels the person as "bad." Judgment condemns and demonizes that person.

In addition to not judging others, we need to stop judging ourselves. When I am feeling loving toward myself, I can feel loving toward others. When I have been stumbling over the lacerating stones of self-hatred and condemnation, I have said some of the meanest things to others that I have ever said. And I've lived to regret every word! I have projected onto others the miserable way that I felt about myself. My daily prayer now is to learn to love myself more so I can love others.

This brings us directly to the issue of conditional love. When I am in judgment, I may withdraw my love from the one I judge, be it myself or another. I place conditions upon love that others must meet. Love then becomes an earned commodity and is operated with an on/off switch.

God does not love like this. God's love is unchanging and without condition. We never have to try to earn God's love or fear its loss.

For Journaling and Reflection...

1. Have you felt loved unconditionally by someone? Describe this relationship.

2. Is there someone whom you love unconditionally? Describe.

3. Do you tend to judge yourself and/or others quickly or harshly? Why or why not?

4. Is it difficult or easy for you to love yourself? If it is difficult, what hinders you? If easy, what helps you?

Affirmation: *I release judgments of myself and others.*

Chapter Fourteen

FEAR

God, what do you want? What more do you want from me? I'm fighting so hard to accept life as it is.

– Paula D'Arcy

I was in my bedroom one evening trying, once again, to straighten out my occasional table when the phone rang. It was my sister, Judy, calling.

"Lyn," she said, "I am calling with a prayer request. Preston just had an emergency appendectomy."

Clouds of doom enveloped me. This is what we had feared most. Preston was my four-year-old great-niece. Her mother and father are missionaries in Lithuania. Preston has a beautiful face with dark brown eyes and a pixie nose. She has a mass of long, black, curly hair. She speaks and sings in several languages. I think she is one of the world's most wonderful children.

Lithuania is part of the old Soviet bloc and is a poor country. Medical care is not up to par with the United States. Although there are many dedicated professionals, money for research and equipment is scarce.

Preston's situation went from bad to worse. My sister called back to report that Preston was being tested for meningitis. I feared for her life. As I tried to pray, I was aware of the fear that was blocking my prayers. I thought about the passage in the Bible that states the Holy Spirit will pray for us when we cannot pray. I also thought about the words of Theresa of Avila to God:

"If this is the way you treat your friends, it is no wonder you have so few of them!"

This passage had always made me chuckle; now I wanted to scream! My prayer was simply, "Please, God! Please, God!"

Ironically, I was scheduled to go to a "Freedom from Fear" workshop on the following Saturday. By this time, the test for meningitis had proved negative, and Preston was slowly recovering. Yet, beloved children die every day! How are we to make sense of it all?

I realized that fear is a reality of life, an emotion that rebels against a possible loss. During the workshop, I offered God my fears and sorrow, my anger. I realized, once again, that I had gained empathy for others through this dark experience.

As I write these words about darkness, thousands of people are dying in Turkey from a devastating earthquake. People are trapped beneath the rubble, crying out for help from others who cannot get there in time. It is very difficult to find any redemption in such a depth of suffering. I cannot explain this, nor do I try.

There have been times when I have wanted to run from faith, but I ask, with Peter, "Lord, to whom shall we go?" I am invited not to run from God but to embrace a God of mystery. I am invited to embrace a life of mystery.

As Fr. Richard Rohr writes in his book, *Job and the Mystery of Suffering*:

"God is not aloof. God is not a mere spectator. God is participating with us. God is not merely tolerating human suffering. Or healing suffering. God is participating with us *in it*. That is what gives believers both meaning and hope."

As I spoke of Preston, I described my fear of extreme loss; yet fear comes to us in many ways. As we stumble along in the dessert, we fear that we may never feel at home again. This brings to mind the words of a friend of mine when she described her necessary breakup with her fiancé:

"It brought up all the 'I'll nevers' – 'I'll never have a partner;' 'I'll never be really happy;' 'I'll never' this; 'I'll never' that."

Many spiritual writers tell us fear is the very opposite of love. It is nearly impossible to be loving when fear controls us. We fear many things: loneliness, humiliation, loss and death. We also fear the desert.

So, it is a courageous thing, an act of faith, when we choose to leave our comfort zones and venture forth into the desert. When we do, we are halfway home.

For Journaling and Reflection...

1. Does fear prevent you from making needed changes in your life? If so, write about how these fears might be faced and overcome.

2. Discuss a fearful time in your life.

3. Re-read Fr. Richard Rohr's statement in the preceding chapter. Respond in your journaling to his thoughts. Is God mysterious to you?

Affirmation: *God holds me in love.*

Chapter Fifteen

BLINDNESS

We witness eternity every day.
— Vic Hummert

*M*y friend tells the amusing story of accompanying her aunt on a tour of Rome. This venerable lady had visited the country several years earlier. While touring in a beautiful, air-conditioned bus, the tour director made an announcement:

"We're almost there! The coliseum is in sight! Get ready!"

My friend's aunt waved her hand and made an announcement of her own:

"Honey, I've already seen it!"

This went on for the whole tour.

"Time for The Church of St. Peter in Chains!"

"I've already seen it!"

Finally, the tour stopped at the Vatican and the aunt rose, regally, from her seat.

"I haven't seen it!" she drawled.

The harassed tour guide quipped:

"Well, my goodness! I thought you'd seen everything."

It is easy to be amused at this lady's blindness, her unwillingness to feast her eyes on treasures simply because she had "seen" them before. But her attitude is a reflection of ours, as we bustle through this world. We don't stop to look because, "We've already seen it."

Buddhists tell us that once language enters our minds we can lose much of our ability to "see." We think that because we can name and describe something, we understand it. But, have we looked with eyes of wonder upon a butterfly and realized that we didn't understand this marvel at all? Have we ever heard a baby's first cry and been struck with astonishment that babies exist at all?

It is also easy to be astonished over the Israelites' behavior in the desert. As I re-read a section of Exodus one morning, the group seemed to be no more than grumbling, squabbling children on a disappointing picnic. Their eyes could see only one thing: "Hey! This isn't what we bargained for!" As God continues to provide for them, raining food from heaven and bringing water from stone, they see only their fear of the future. And, yes, they are us!

As I discussed this chapter on blindness with a friend, the subject of prejudice came up. She made an interesting observation:

"I wonder how many wonderful relationships we miss because someone is the wrong color, doesn't look right to our eyes, or is judged to be too different from us?"

Not only is prejudice a moral failing, but it is also something that can cheat us out of some great relationships in life.

As I sat down to write this chapter on blindness, I was frustrated because I had misplaced my glasses. Considering the irony of this, I could not help but smile. I realized that as I age I must accept new limitations, whether I like it or not. But some limitations are strictly self-imposed. Blinded by preconceptions and fears, I can miss the miracles. Yes, I can even miss the water that comes pouring from the stone.

For Journaling and Reflection...

1. Do you feel comfortable in unfamiliar situations and around unknown people? Why or why not?

2. Look closely at something in nature (plant, tree, bird, pet). Describe it in detail. Notice the way you are observing it with "new eyes." Practice seeing your world with "new eyes."

3. Do you use TV or other things to insulate yourself from seeing the real world? If so, why?

Affirmation: *Open my eyes that I may see.*

Chapter Sixteen

Holding onto Stones: The Forgiveness Factor

*Being ignorant of our true selves means that we only
continue blindly along, assuming that our well-meaning
conscious personality expresses the truth of what we
really are.*
— William A. Miller

heresa and Mark married when each was twenty.
Theresa seemed to be the stronger, and definitely the
more outspoken, of the pair. They settled into a small house, and
in three years had welcomed two beautiful daughters.

Yes, life seemed a little burdensome, with so much work with
the babies and Mark pulling overtime, but, as Theresa said, "That's
just the way life is." She no longer bothered with her appearance
very much (too tired), and he didn't come home right after work,
but "marriage was like that."

Things went along "fine" until the day Mark asked for a divorce. He was having an affair with another woman. Theresa
changed that day. Anyone who was observing the situation would

certainly give her permission to be in a rage. She had been abandoned with her children. She quickly enlisted the help of the entire neighborhood to testify for her in court. The judge told Mark to turn over most of his monthly salary to her.

There was just one major problem remaining: Theresa's rage was never to leave her for the rest of her life.

She never lost the opportunity to talk at length about what an unfaithful bum Mark was. Every situation with the children became a reason to inflict pain. She "forgot" that he was coming to get them on a particular day. She "forgot" to tell Mark about ballet recitals and ball games. Her children lived in confusion.

Eventually, the girls began having a lot of problems. By the time they were teenagers, one had gotten pregnant and the other was heavily into drugs. Theresa told everyone, "What do you expect? Their father abandoned them!"

Theresa was not even aware that she was perpetuating the pain of all concerned by refusing to forgive. Was Mark innocent? Of course not! What he did may seem unforgivable to many of us, but the question becomes, "Who was harmed by this lack of forgiveness?" It seems that everyone was, especially Theresa herself.

Forgiveness is a tricky issue, and I did not write this chapter to instruct everyone to forgive everything. I have not had to suffer the terrible things at the hands of another that many have. Only the wounded person knows if forgiveness is a viable option for him/her at a particular point in time. I only know that forgiveness brings healing, especially for the one who forgives.

Scott Peck, writing in *The Road Less Traveled*, gave a definition of forgiveness that I have used in my own life: "the refusal to take revenge." I have found this definition most useful when I perceive that someone has hurt my son or my husband. These hurts are the hardest for me to forgive. The refusal to take revenge means that I no longer plot fantasy retaliations in my head! Since I no longer feed energy into hating someone, my energy can be used to bring some positive things into the world.

If you want to forgive someone, do not decide that your feelings are the barometer of whether you can forgive or whether you have forgiven. I suggest that you use as your measure your "intent to forgive." I have found this prayer very useful, and I pray it often:

The Forgiveness Prayer

Lord, I truly want to forgive _____*.*
Please remove any obstacles that are blocking this forgiveness.
Please fill my heart with peace concerning _____*.*

This prayer is also useful when we insert our own names. So often it is ourselves that we cannot forgive.

I once talked with a friend who had lost thirty pounds. She spoke of the way in which her energy level had risen.

"Just think!" she said. "It's like putting down a thirty-pound load that you have been carrying every minute!"

Perhaps, in your life and mine, forgiveness can be just like this. We can put down heavy burdens that God does not intend for us to carry.

For Journaling and Reflection...

1. What do you need to forgive yourself for? Can you forgive yourself now, using The Forgiveness Prayer?

2. Is there someone in your life against whom you hold a grudge? Would you like to forgive that person?

3. Has practicing forgiveness enhanced your life? In what ways?

Affirmation: *May I put down my burdens.*

Chapter Seventeen

UNWORTHINESS

We do not see our size. We do not view ourselves with accuracy. We are far larger, far more marvelous, far more deeply and consistently creative than we recognize or know.
— Julia Cameron

The Israelites almost didn't have a leader to take them out of Egypt. If you believe, as I do, that God doesn't force anyone to do anything, then you will understand my point when you reread certain portions of Exodus. Moses asked:

"Who am I, that I should go to Pharaoh and lead the Israelites out of Egypt?"

He asked later:

"If they ask me, 'What is his name,' what will I tell them?"

Still later he questioned God:

"Suppose they will not believe me or listen to my plea?"

Well, you get the idea. Moses exhibited great unworthiness in the face of an undeniable call from God.

Once I was telling an acquaintance that I was training to be a Eucharistic minister (someone who serves communion). She held up her hands to stop my words and said, "Oh, I'm not worthy to do that! Just not worthy!" The look in her eyes was one of sheer disapproval. She looked at me as if to say, "Surely, you don't think *you're* worthy!"

I felt confusion! Frankly, I had not thought about being worthy or unworthy. The priest had just said he really needed people to do this job, and I had volunteered.

We must not demean ourselves by buying in to the notion of our being unworthy. This sort of wretched perception about ourselves deadens our hearts to God's call. It neutralizes us. It disempowers us.

Jesus seemed to delight in choosing the "unworthy" as his disciples. This practice was a continuation of his desire to set the world on its head, to make people see in a new way. He chose Peter, despite his bad temper and impulsiveness; unpopular tax collectors who were hated by everyone; and the doubting Thomas. These were the people he chose to help carry out his ministry.

Even such a towering figure as John the Baptist felt his unworthiness. He stated humbly:

"One is following me whose sandal strap I am not fit to fasten."

Yet John overcame his fears and was chosen to baptize Jesus himself! In John's life we truly see that *willingness* in the face of unworthy feelings can change the world.

Moses finally understood that he was the facilitator of the loving power of God, and he went on to save God's people from bondage. It is the same with us: We can be instruments for the Spirit, despite our unworthiness. I believe that, in God's eyes, we are all worthy to bring God's light into the world.

For Journaling and Reflection...

1. Is "unworthiness" or low self-esteem an issue with you? Why or why not?

2. List methods that could raise low self-esteem. (Prayer, therapy, setting goals, etc.) Are there methods that have helped you in the past? Try to revisit them.

3. How would you feel if you were Moses? How would you respond to God's call?

Affirmation: God finds me worthy of all good things.

Chapter Eighteen

SYNTHESIS

We are terribly afraid of admitting that we have been
wrong, of admitting weakness; yet, only when we can
does the light flow in like a pardon.   – May Sarton

*L*et us not become discouraged with ourselves as we un-
cover the stumbling stones in our lives. We are all human; therefore we are subject to judgments, fear, blindness, non-
forgiveness and unworthiness. It is our courageous willingness to
face these weaknesses and wounds that marks us as spiritual pilgrims in the desert – pilgrims who want to reach a better place.

Take some time, as you re-read your journal for Part Three, to
consider whether the foregoing foibles are obstacles in your path.
Give yourself much time and care as you work to remove these bar-
riers to a fuller life in the Spirit.

Do not hesitate to seek out spiritual directors, good friends or any
good listeners, to "sound out" some of your ideas and feelings. Protect this process from those who would "throw cold water on it."

For Journaling and Reflection...

Re-read and respond to your journaling pages for this part of the book. You may want to illustrate some of your insights through drawing or painting.

Affirmation: *God removes all obstacles.*

Morning is Forgiveness

Forgiveness is found
In this mysterious hour,
With each turning
Of the Earth
Toward Light
And Light softens
... Softens the darkness ...
And darkness opens
Bit by bit
... Opens the gift ...
Of morning.

Oh, Light, do come and call me
From this still, black night.
Light, you must ...
Wake me and
Wash me.
Then, nourish me with your Gentleness.

Again and again,
You carry me barefoot
Through the wet grass
To a bench where I sit.

Now, you hand me the cup
Filled with birdsong,
Urging me ...
"Drink it! Drink it!"

I sip from the cup
... Swallow your Mercy ...
So warm,
Golden and fine.
Oh, Radiant Light!
I'm turning toward you,
Bowing
Before such Tenderness.

— Laurie Trumps

PART IV
A NEW LAND

Chapter Nineteen

SELF-ACCEPTANCE

Darling, the body is a great house; every morning,
someone new arrives. — Jelaluddin Rumi

*N*ow that we have made our way across the dry, barren desert, we can rest for a while and savor some of the rewards that we find as we enter this new land of hope and promise. The first reward I want to discuss is self-acceptance, as illustrated in the story which follows.

After Preston, my great-niece, recovered from her illness, my husband and I were able to visit her and her family in Lithuania. We stayed with them in their home.

Since my sister was also visiting, there were five adults and two children – and only one shower. This is not at all unusual in most parts of the world. It required scheduling, especially because the hot water would run out frequently.

One morning I postponed my shower and played with Preston, all morning, in her room. We read *If You Give a Moose a Muffin* thirty-seven times and acted out scenes from *The Rescuers*. Lunchtime was approaching, and Preston wanted to play one more game.

"Preston," I said, "I am yuck! I need to wash my hair, take a shower! I haven't even brushed my teeth!"

She chuckled, and I checked to see if there was any hot water.

The next morning, I went into her room to give her hugs and kisses before going down to breakfast. Her merry dark eyes twinkled.

"Are you 'yuck' this morning?" she asked.

This little linguist had acquired a new word, and she was delighted to use it.

I paused. A part of me wanted to say:

"Yes, Preston, I am 'yuck.' I am like Paul in the Bible: I don't do the things I should and I do the things I should not. I am moody, I lack self-discipline, and I am not as grateful as I should be much of the time."

I never want to ignore or downplay any of my actions or attitudes that I know to be destructive. But I don't think this is my usual problem. My problem is that I am constantly bothered by my lack of perfection – and I realize that this is not a healthy attitude.

I have noticed that listing all my faults and berating myself rarely makes me better; it only makes me depressed and lethargic. Only by seeking to love myself, as well as others, more do I improve. It is then that I am able to look at all my faults and to find the gift in them. I then seek to mold them with love. Only in believing that I am worthy of God's love do I have the courage to change, the will to walk a path that is ever new.

So I responded:

"No, Preston. I am in pretty good shape this morning. Now, how about that hug and kiss?"

For Journaling and Reflection...

1. List the things you would like to change about yourself. Then, list the positive aspects of each fault.

Example: I'm messy. Gift: This could be interpreted as I'm spontaneous and creative.

Example: I'm stingy. Gift: This could mean I'm careful and responsible.

2. Write a prayer of thanksgiving for who you are. The harder it is to write this, the more you need to do it. Read the prayer out loud daily during this week.

3. Sometime during the week find a friend who can tell you your gifts and strengths. Do the same for that person.

Affirmation: *I am fully accepted as I am.*

Chapter Twenty

SEEING GOD

*So my heart rejoices, my soul delights, my body too
will rest secure.*   (Psalm 16:9)

If we have truly absorbed the gifts of the desert we have
the opportunity to see God all around us in our everyday
lives. A simple walk can be a communion with the Spirit.

The route I take when I walk is several miles. In the beginning, it takes me up a busy highway. This part resembles everyday life, as I dodge cars, check behind me, and steel myself for
the challenge.

Then I turn off onto a much quieter road. I begin to tune in to
the signs and smells around me. Passing an oil company entrance,
I usually see people going in and out, some smiling, some
resigned. On my left are cattle of many different colors.

Then a surprise: There are three new baby lambs in a small
front pasture. They kick up their feet and run with pure joy. The
breeze is soft as I pass the little park where two young women are

playing tennis. On the swings, a mother sits motionless with her daughter of about six, talking quietly. The ditch adjoining the park is filled with honeysuckle. The air is sweet.

My breathing becomes regular. I decide to clear my mind. If I am not careful, I can waste my walk in brooding thoughts. I breathe in ... God. I breathe out ... self. I do this over and over. A friend (or former friend) who is angry with me comes into my thoughts. I send her a blessing (with difficulty) and work to clear my mind again.

A left turn, and I am in front of the new home of a retired couple. The setting fills me with peace. Every blade of grass is clipped, every leaf swept, pink and white impatiens bloom beside the mailbox. The "lady of the house" is out watering. She gives me a friendly "Hello."

Coming up next is an elementary school; echoes of children's voices can almost be heard as I pass by.

It is easy to meditate on how quickly life goes by. Moving through space has calmed me. My mind is clearer as the rhythm of my steps joins with my breathing. I smell the rich, spicy aroma of pines. I hear the peck-pock, peck-pock of a red-headed woodpecker.

Once I saw a tiny baby possum on the grassy edge of the road. His little mouth was stained from eating the berries he held in his minuscule paws. I was touched with wonder.

My body begins to be a moving meditation as I visualize myself walking into a quiet pool of pure, cool water. This is God's spirit. I am in the Spirit, and it is in me.

For Journaling and Reflection...

1. How do you calm your mind and body?

2. Does nature or some other aid help you to feel closer to God? How?

3. What gifts are you seeking in *your* new land? Describe some of them in detail.

4. Describe God as you perceive God at this moment.

Affirmation: *God is present in all things.*

Chapter Twenty-one

INNER KNOWING

The spider as an artist
Has never been employed
Though his surpassing merit
Is freely certified
        – Emily Dickinson

*E*arly one morning I set out for a walk, and I noticed shiny white glistenings everywhere! Looking closer, I saw they were tiny spider webs that had been attached to every twig and blade of grass as far as the eye could see.

The entire front pasture was coated with the sparkling shimmer of dew that had settled on the webs. I did not see the spiders that had been busily working all night. I stood in awe at the sheer multitude of spider webs. As I took my walk I saw them everywhere.

A few days later, they were gone.

What voice had spoken, propelling all the little spiders, as one, to labor through the night? A deep, mysterious force of Spirit had called out the steps to an ancient dance.

When I thought about this inner knowing, I smiled, then began thinking about the pecan trees. A grove of these trees is just across the street from my house. The pecan tree is notoriously stubborn about putting out its leaves in the spring. For this reason, it is rarely caught by a late frost. It seems as though the wily pecan tree has read the warning: Bloom when all danger of frost is past!

It would be nice if we human beings could wait to bloom until all danger of frost is past, but I know that our unfolding and the blooming of our authentic lives will begin in God's time. Our greening begins with the water from stones in the desert – and we can never again be the little seed, safely hidden in the earth. However, we can practice healthy self-protection. We do not need to expose our soft and vulnerable new growth to those who would blow icy winds upon it.

And I know that, if I continue to listen, I will hear wisdom's inner voice, and so will you. This is the voice of Spirit and wisdom that has already led us out of the desert. It calls out the steps to the dance, the beautiful dance of life.

For Journaling and Reflection...

1. Do you trust your intuition? Why or why not? Explain.

2. How could you take the time and what would help you to "get in touch" with your own wisdom? (Examples: Solitude, talking to a certain friend, meditation, music ...)

3. Does your body tell you when you are hurt, overtired, or sad? (For example, sadness may cause tenseness in a part of the body.)

4. If you are in a sad or trying time, can you find the lesson in it? Do you need to discuss this with someone? (Often, voicing our feelings gains for us greater inner clarity.)

Affirmation: *Inner wisdom lights my path.*

Chapter Twenty-two

BEING HOME

As I evaluated (my patient's) energy, I realized that
he was a professional do-gooder to everyone but
himself.   – Caroline Myss

*I*n the course of preparing this book to be published, I was explaining to my editor what it feels like to me "to be home."

"Have you ever felt a special way, perhaps at the end of a retreat, when the good silence fills your soul, and you feel loved and safe? And then you know that your little life is not an accident of nature, but is held firmly in God's hand? And all seems right with the world? This is what I think of as being home," I explained.

He smiled, as warmth and comprehension filled his eyes. Yes, he knew that feeling.

Of course, life is not a retreat, but an immersion! We cannot live alone on the mountaintop with God. However, I believe we can experience this certainty of God's love and a sureness of our place almost every day if we will allow ourselves the time and space to do so.

Once I heard a group of women discussing what types of places and activities nourished their inner growth and relationship with the Divine. Their answers were varied:

"Quiet."

"Solitude."

"Time for prayer."

"Being around positive, spiritual people."

"Good reading."

"Spending time in nature."

"Resting, just being, not doing."

"Drawing."

"Journaling."

"Listening to beautiful music."

Then they were asked by the facilitator:

"What portion of each day do you spend doing these types of nourishing activities?"

A few people, usually those with empty nests like mine, could claim at least some time each day, perhaps an hour, spent doing these things that nourish the soul. Others revealed that weeks would go by for them without quiet or solitude or other things they deemed important.

When things get quiet, we have to look inside. It is not easy. The rush to fill the silence and to avoid the inner chaos is almost unbearable at times. Sometimes I find it very difficult to sit and contemplate. (I can read for hours on end, but that is not the same thing.)

Our lives have gotten so busy. I once saw a report that stated technology has actually made us more rushed. Our expectations now are that we can do dozens of things every day.

Why are we rushing around so hard? Do our children really need to do so many things? Couldn't they just hang around at home more? Couldn't they just be with us, sometimes?

If they get bored, so what? Boredom is not a disease that kills; it can actually help us to grow. I was seldom bored as a child because I could spend a day with old bricks making a house, or playing pretend, or making up stories. (There wasn't much else to do on those long summer days. And if you told adults you were bored, they might give you a chore to do!)

Walking a path that keeps us connected with the Spirit prepares us for desert times, but it also enables us to sing and dance now, living at home in Paradise. In his book, *The Dragon Doesn't Live Here Anymore*, Alan Cohen delights me by writing:

"The reward of the adventure of life is freedom ... not to be found where we fantasized it to be. We needed to learn, like our old friend, Dorothy from Kansas, that there's no place like home, because there is no place *but* home.... God is everywhere (and) Love fills all space."

For Journaling and Reflection...

1. What activities make you happy and allow you to grow?

2. Can you make plans to engage in these activities daily or weekly? Specifically, how do you do this?

3. Is there someone whose sense of peace and love you admire? Journal about that person. Can you talk to this person about his/her spiritual practices?

4. What is "home" for you? You may want to make a list of adjectives like safe, warm, etc.

Affirmation: *I am home.*

Chapter Twenty-three

LISTEN, LISTEN, LISTEN

*Every now and again something happens in our lives
to challenge us, or to make us change direction....
Suddenly it happens, and life is never the same again.*
                                                        – David Adam

We are a results-oriented society. We are doers! As we come close to the end of our journey together, what have we done?

Hopefully, we have opened our hearts a little. We have released fear a little. We know our own hearts better. We have loved ourselves and others a little more. We have learned not to run screaming into the night when desert times approach.

And hopefully, we have taken time to look at those things in life that we cannot change and those things that we can.

The end of a journey is only another beginning, so I would like to share a story about "listening" that may be helpful to you as you continue on your unique road.

A lady I know well, Nancy, rose early one humid summer morning to prepare her notes for the summer school class she was teaching at the University of Louisiana at Lafayette. As she sipped her tea, her thoughts drifted to the Sisters of Charity mission that Mother Teresa established in Lafayette. Then a voice came to her clearly:

"Go and visit the sisters this morning."

Nancy argued with the voice:

"I can't go there this morning. I have to get ready to teach at 11 o'clock."

However, the voice repeated its message, so she got her purse and left for the mission. When she knocked on the door, one of the nuns said, "I'm coming! We've been waiting for you!"

"Well," Nancy said hesitantly when the door opened, "can I do something for you this morning? Do you need something?"

The tiny sister in her blue and white sari-styled habit replied:

"Yes, we really need to go to the post office to get some stamps so that we can write and thank all the people who have helped us get started here. Just let me get my purse."

Nancy drove the sister to the post office, and they waited in line. The voice returned:

"Pay for the stamps."

"Sister," Nancy said, "I would be happy to pay for your stamps."

"Thank you so much, my dear. That will certainly help."

Once back in the car, Nancy found out that the sister really needed to go to the grocery store. They traveled there, and she followed her as she placed a few simple items in their basket. When they approached the checkout lane, the voice returned.

"Pay for the groceries."

Nancy didn't argue. She stepped up and paid for the food and was again thanked warmly by the little nun.

The pair parked in front of the mission house and walked to the door. As they did, Nancy realized why she had been called to the aid of the sisters on this very morning. She turned to the nun and asked gently:

"You don't have any money, do you?"

The sister opened her large black purse. It was completely empty. She smiled.

"The Lord always provides," the sister said.

Nancy made it back to campus in time to teach her class. She remembers the events of that day with affection and awe.

It seems rather dramatic to claim that God is so clearly speaking to us. Yet how can we deny a story such as this? For the purpose of our healing is not just for ourselves, but for the world. There is ample evidence that the Spirit is trying to break through to us all the time, however, we are too busy and distracted to listen! Let us listen closer and hear with new ears.

For Journaling and Reflection...

1. Would you have listened to the inner voice as Nancy did? Why or why not?

2. To what special form of service do you feel called?

3. Are there circumstances in your life that prevent you from serving fully as you would like? Can you change any of these circumstances?

Affirmation: *God removes all obstacles.*

Chapter Twenty-four

SYNTHESIS

*Ideally, (the inner journey) ends quietly, with a new
wisdom and a coming to oneself that releases great
power.*   – Gerald O'Collins

*A*s I write these lines, it is the beginning of the fourth
week of Advent. The Magi are making their long so-
journ across the burning desert, following the star. I am struck
again by how often the desert journey is required to truly reach
the Christ.

The Magi sought the blessings on the other side of the desert,
and so do we. I believe these gifts exist in abundance. They are
the little bits of heaven that we can taste nearly every day, if we
choose to.

Once the experience of wilderness and desolation moves us
past our own small egos, we can truly learn what it means to love
ourselves and others. Self-acceptance becomes possible as we
understand our humble but vital place in God's great plan. As

we release our rigidity and perfectionism, we can open ourselves to the beauty all around us – in the natural world and in the amazing glory and diversity of the human race.

Like Nancy, who helped the Sisters of Charity, answering God's call on an ordinary summer morning, we can listen to God's voice and strengthen our inner knowing. We will help others with joy and gratitude, no longer striving in exhaustion to earn the love that we already possess. Oh, we will fail, we will sometimes be confused, and we will say and do things we regret. But we will possess more wisdom and power and we will be armed with new spiritual tools. We will be at home with the One who always accepts us as we are.

Yes, we will enter the desert again, for life is cyclic. Once we have tasted "arriving at home," though, we are never the same. We cannot forget for long the gentle care of the One who brought us through the wasteland.

For Journaling and Reflection...

Take some time now and in the days to come to review your journaling pages for Part 4, *A New Land*. If you have left blank spaces between your journal entries, you can write about any changes that you are experiencing. Note how God is speaking to you and the ways in which you can nurture your communication with God.

In the future, I invite you to review all the journaling you have done while reading *Water From Stones*. Perhaps, you will discover that you are more awake, more loving, and that you feel a new sense of control and willingness to make needed changes in your life. As we welcome God more fully into our daily lives we will, as the Serenity Prayer teaches, have the courage to change the things we can.

Affirmation: *I rest in God's will.*

Water from Stones

"What are stones?" the woman asked,
holding the smooth river stone aloft in her hand.
"Are they the bad things in life,
Or the good?"

"How to tell?" we all agreed,
"When the best can come (ah, with a price) from the place
We called the worst!
How to tell?"

"Stones are smoothed by water," she said.
Light was streaming against her auburn hair
"Even the roughest stones are smoothed,
As the water flows."

"Stones purify the water
They make it clear.
It seems that stones need water,
And water needs stones."

She lifted once again the blue river rock.
On it, she had written,
"Awareness."
I placed it in my little fountain,
And I see it every day.

— Lyn Holley Doucet

Epilogue

*Then Moses led the people out of the camp to
meet God....* (Exodus 19:17)

A psychologist was conducting a workshop, and she
passed out a questionnaire to the group that asked,
among other things, "Do you consider yourself to be in a time of
transition?"

Nearly everyone there answered, "Yes." Some of the partici-
pants were in their thirties, others in their sixties. Yet most felt
themselves to be in a time of transition.

The psychologist concluded that it was helpful to look upon
life itself as transition, the great transition – a long journey filled
with many smaller leavings, deserts and homecomings.

Perhaps another useful way of looking upon transitions is to
consider the healing that takes place in our "desert times" and in
our homecomings. Healing is available to all, just as living water
was accessible to the Samaritan woman at the well. The question
becomes this:

"What does healing mean for me? In my 'desert times,' what
have I learned that will facilitate my healing?"

You have read stories about people who learned they could not control many things in their lives. Women who learned that no matter how hard they tried to be perfect all of their expectations could not be met. We have talked about new ways of seeing and of releasing judgments, but the question remains:

"What is healing for you? What is being healed in your life? What stubborn wounds still need to be healed?"

Years ago I learned of a beneficial way of dealing with the continuing hurts in my life. (I seemed to be meeting the same demons at every turn in the road.) A friend told me:

"Yes, you do keep dealing with the same issues. But you are spiraling up, not returning to where you were. You are dealing with things on a higher and higher level."

Well, this statement gave me much hope. Healing can come in great gulps of living water, or in a small trickle of the clearest, smallest mountain stream. And healing can come from a tiny, single drop on the driest, most painful place.

Jesuit mystic Anthony DeMello once described us all as fish swimming in the ocean, looking for the ocean. We do this as we say, "Where's God? Where's God?"

We are swimming in God!

For God is love, and this is our truth: We have been surrounded and supported by Love since the moment of our conception and even before. We are truly spirit as well as flesh, and Love is our reality.

Suggestions for Group Use of Water from Stones

The book, *Water from Stones*, is ideally suited for group use.

If meetings are monthly, the group may want to read two or three chapters of the book during a one-month period. If meetings are weekly, then the group may want to discuss one chapter at a time.

Group members should bring their journals to the meetings. One member of the group can lead the discussion by reading the journaling questions aloud and asking the members to share thoughts from their journals.

Good rules for group sharing should be followed: confidentiality; patient, active listening; and releasing the desire to "fix" others or to give advice.

You may begin your session with the Prayer Ritual on the following page.

Prayer Ritual

If *Water from Stones* is utilized in a group setting, this ritual can be used before discussions begin. It will serve to calm and center the group and to invite the Spirit of God into the meeting.

Setting: The following can be used to enhance the needed sacred space: a clay pot filled with sand, rocks of various types, an opened Bible, assorted lit candles, and a bowl of water.

Appoint a leader and two readers from the group. This can be done just before the ritual begins.

Music: A soft recording of ambient music can be played, or songs such as *Hosea, Peace is Flowing Like a River,* or *You Are Mine* can be played or sung as an opening to the ritual.

Readings: (Read slowly, with feeling.)
Reader One: Romans 15:5-7 (Truncated) May God, the source of all patience and encouragement, enable you to live in perfect harmony with one another.... Accept one another...as Christ has accepted you.

(Pause and reflect for a few moments.)
Reader Two: Ultimate freedom requires an acceptance of oneself as coming from God, going to God, and being with God. It includes a sense of well-being, self-identity and basic peace. A person who is thus free can in peace answer the questions, "Who am I? Where am I going?" (from *Spiritual Freedom*)

(Pause and reflect for a few moments.)

Candle Ceremony:

Leader: As we hold this candle, let us contemplate the flame within our own hearts. Do we have fires within that set us aflame with enthusiasm? Do we have fires within that destroy? Holy Spirit, touch us and teach us to discern in our own hearts.

Soft music may be played as the candle slowly moves from one person to another. The person holding the candle observes a special meditation time, searching his/her heart. Take your time with this part of the ceremony. Observe silence.

As the candle returns to the leader, she/he places it on the table.

Leader: We will speak of desert times.

She/he slowly filters sand between fingers.

(Pause)

Reader One: We will search for clear water.

She/he filters water between fingers.

(Pause)

Leader: Spirit of Truth and Joy, we go forth with the confidence that you are with us at all times. You help us to show love and acceptance to others and to ourselves. Let your light shine within us and illuminate our hearts. Amen.

Note: Feel free to adapt this ceremony to your own use. Readings from other books can be used. Props other than the candle are optional. Keep the ceremony simple, allowing silence and time to center the group.

Bibliography

Adam, David. *A Desert in the Ocean*. New York: Paulist Press, 2000.

Barry, William. *Paying Attention to God*. Notre Dame, Indiana: Ave Maria Press, 1990.

Cameron, Julia. *The Right to Write*. New York: Penguin Putnam, 1998.

Cohen, Alan. *The Dragon Doesn't Live Here Anymore*. New York: Ballantine Books, 1990.

Coyle, Neva. *Whatever Happened to the Real Me?* Ann Arbor, Mich.: Servant Publications, 1997.

D'Arcy, Paula. *Gift of the Red Bird*. New York: The Crossroad Publishing Company, 1997.

DeMello, Anthony. *Walking on Water*. New York: The Crossroad Publishing Company, 1998.

Dickinson, Emily. *Collected Poems*. New York: Barnes and Nobel Books, 1993.

Duerk, Judith. *Circle of Stones*. Philadelphia: Innisfree Press, Inc., 1999.

Eliot, T.S. *The Wasteland and Other Poems*. San Diego: Harcourt, Brace and Company, 1962.

English, John J. *Spiritual Freedom*. Chicago: Loyola Press, 1995.

Froehle, Virginia Ann. *Loving Yourself More*. Notre Dame, Indiana: Ave Maria Press, 1993.

Gibran, Kahlil. *The Prophet*. New York: Alfred A. Knopf, 1993.

Hanh, Thich Nhat. *Being Peace*. Berkeley: Parallax Press, 1996.

Hummert, Vic. *Tersely Yours, Vol. III*. Lafayette, La: Earth Literacy Press, 1998.

Johnson, Paul. *Quest for God*. New York: HarperCollins, 1997.

Kushner, Harold. *How Good Do We Have to Be?* Boston: Little Brown and Company, 1996.

Miller, William A. *Make Friends With Your Shadow*. Minneapolis: Augsburg Fortress Publishing, 1980.

Myss, Caroline. *Anatomy of the Spirit*. New York: Random House, Inc., 1996.

Norris, Kathleen. *Amazing Grace*. New York: Penguin Putnam, Inc., 1998.

Nouwen, Henri J.M. *The Inner Voice of Love*. New York: Doubleday Books, 1998.

O'Collins, Gerald. *The Second Journey*. New York: Paulist Press, 1978.

Peck, Scott. *The Road Less Traveled*. New York: Simon and Schuster, 1978.

Rhodes, Tricia McCary. *The Soul at Rest*. Minneapolis: Bethany House Publishers, 1996.

Rohr, Richard and Ebert, Andreas. *Discovering the Enneagram*. New York: Crossroad Publishing, 1999.

Rohr, Richard. *Job and the Mystery of Suffering*. New York: Crossroad Publishing, 1998.

Rumi, Jelaluddin *Love is a Stranger*. New York: Random House, Inc., 1996.

Rupp, Joyce. *The Cup of Life*. Notre Dame, Ind.: Ave Maria Press, 1997.

Wiederkehr, Macrina. *A Tree Full of Angels*. San Francisco: HarperCollins, 1988.

Index

About the Author...

LYN HOLLEY DOUCET is an educator, writer and speaker who has been involved in church ministries for many years. She teaches religion, leads a musical ensemble, and is a nationally published composer with Unity Music Press.

Mrs. Doucet reads and writes avidly in the areas of creativity, self-help, spirituality and psychology.

She has a Master of Education degree from the University of Louisiana at Lafayette and a Bachelor of Arts degree in speech and English from Louisiana State University. She has spent much of her life as a professional educator working with handicapped and troubled children in special school settings.

She and her teaching partner, Donna Hayes, lead women's retreats on "The Christian Spiritual Journey" and "Healing Through Prayer." Mrs. Doucet is a practicing Catholic and is active in the Theresians movement and in the National Association of Pastoral Musicians.

A convert from the Methodist faith, she is from a family that now includes Baptists, Methodists, Episcopalians and Catholics.

As a child she lived on a farm near Bastrop, La. Today she lives in the country near Lafayette, La., with her husband, Dee Doucet. They have one son, Jacques, who is a sportscaster. She enjoys her plants and animals (including pigs), as well as frequent walks and daily writing.

Inspirational Books
from
ACADIAN HOUSE
PUBLISHING

Freedom From Fear
A Way Through The Ways of Jesus The Christ

Everyone at one time or another feels fear, guilt, worry and shame. But when these emotions get out of control they can enslave a person, literally taking over his or her life. In this 142-page hardcover book, the author suggests that the way out of this bondage is prayer, meditation and faith in God and His promise of salvation. The author points to the parables in the Gospels as Jesus' antidote to fears of various kinds, citing the parables of the prodigal son, the good Samaritan, and the widow and the judge. Exercises at the end of each chapter help make the book's lessons all the more real and useful. (Author: Francis Vanderwall. ISBN: 0-925417-34-3. Price: $14.95)

The Forgotten Hero of My Lai
The Hugh Thompson Story

A 248-page hardcover book that tells the story of the U.S. Army helicopter pilot who risked his life to rescue South Vietnamese civilians and to put a stop to the My Lai massacre during the Vietnam War in 1968. An inspiring story about the courage to do the right thing under extremely difficult circumstances, regardless of the consequences. Illustrated with maps and photos. (Author: Trent Angers. ISBN: 0-925417-33-5. Price: $22.95)

The Elephant Man
A Study in Human Dignity

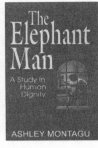

The Elephant Man is a 138-page softcover book whose first edition inspired the movie and the Tony Award-winning play by the same name. This fascinating story, which has touched the hearts of readers throughout the world for over a century, is now complete with the publication of this, the Third Edition. Illustrated with photos and drawings of The Elephant Man. (Author: Ashley Montagu. ISBN: 0-925417-17-3. Price: $12.95.)

Why Men Watch Football

Why Men Watch Football is a 172-page hardcover book that is the definitive work on a subject that millions have asked themselves at one time or another: Why *do* men watch football so much? The book is a serious study of the male psyche, and it also has a humorous side. Illustrated with photos. (Author: Bob Andelman. ISBN: 0-925417-14-9. Price: $14.95.)

Water From Stones
An Inner Journey

Water From Stones is a 128-page hardcover book that is designed to serve as an instrument of healing, renewal and enlightenment for those who are seeking to walk a spiritual path. It is a book for those who are willing to take positive steps toward a more meaningful, more joyful life. The author maintains that the events and circumstances that test our hearts and spirits can bring forth our greatest gifts. She points out that spiritual and psychological healing comes to us as we learn and accept what she refers to as "the lessons of the desert." (Author: Lyn Holley Doucet. ISBN: 0-925417-40-8. Price: $12.95.)

TO ORDER, list the books you wish to purchase along with the corresponding cost of each. Add $3 per book for shipping & handling. Louisiana residents add 7½% tax to the cost of the books. Mail your order and check or credit card authorization (VISA/MC/AmEx) to: Acadian House Publishing, Dept. B-34, Box 52247, Lafayette, LA 70505. Or call (800) 850-8851.